Breakthrough to Success

Ron Stubbs

Dedication

To my wife, my partner and

Love of my life

Jeanie

I found my bottle in the sand

To my daughters, Heather and Mackenzie

May your dreams only be eclipsed by your reality

To you, the reader

For allowing me to reach my dreams

And Kelley…thanks so much

Contact Ron Stubbs

Island Productions

360-387-1197

Copyright Island Productions 2004-2015

All rights reserved.

Printed in the United States of America.

Table of Contents

Introduction		1
Chapter One	The Journey	5
Chapter Two	Values/Balance/Awareness	13
Chapter Three	Release	25
Chapter Four	7 Steps to Loving Yourself	29
Chapter Five	Attraction & Creating	37
Chapter Six	Map Of Reality	41
Chapter Seven	Creating New Reality	59
Chapter Eight	Easy	65
Chapter Nine	Money	69
Chapter Ten	Review Your Changes	83
Chapter Eleven	Roadmap to Success	89

A very special message from the desk of Ron Stubbs

Hello, my friend, and welcome to Breakthrough to Success.

Have you ever wanted something; whatever it was, so much that in your mind, you could touch it, taste it, smell it, feel it; make it so real that it seemed to be right in front of you but seemed like only a dream.. Then... as if by "magic" it appeared? Congratulations my friend, you have discovered **Manifestation.**

In life we have many opportunities presented to us each and every day. Sometimes we seize these fleeting flashes of brilliance; other times they seem to slip from our grasp. Perhaps, if you are like me and don't write them down they can be lost in vacuum of space forever.

The book which you are now holding in your hands is unique in the fact that the words and exercises within this and pages have the ability to transform you and change your life.

They are a roadmap, a guide for a successful life change. Not meant to show you an exact way to your destination but rather a purposeful view intended to open your eyes to the world you've created and provide a pathway to change.

Imagine something with me for just a moment:. Everything that you have experienced in life up to now is just that---an experience.

You are free to move on from who you were, what you have done, who you have been in your past to becoming who you want to be, doing what you want to do and designing where you want your life to go---if you simply recognize that the potential for change exists within you.

In this book you will find ways to change your ideas, outlook and behaviors. Ways to open the box of your mind and let those rays of brilliance come out and play.

There may even be some information and ideas that may turn you in directions that you have never considered before.

That is the beauty of Breakthrough to Success.

No longer are you locked into performing a play that has been written for you in which you have no say. Now you can be the playwright, director, actor and supporting cast all rolled into one.

Your future has never been as ripe for opportunity and change as right now. That is as long as you begin to put into practice what you are about to read and actually commit yourself to acting upon the advice given in this book and doing the work.

If you intend to get the most you can from this book, here's my advice to you:

Go through it a few times, wear it out, mark up these pages, highlight special passages, bend down the corners of the pages, use paper clips to mark special sections, clip out a great idea and post in on your fridge or bathroom mirror.

Maybe you'll photocopy some pages to pass along to friends and family or tear them out to carry with you, reminding you of the awesomely powerful person you have become.

After you have read the book, cover to cover, done the exercises, gotten unbelievable value from it, used it and abused it, turned it into a shambles, you'll probably want to go buy a second copy for yourself to keep in pristine condition and 10-20 more copies to pass along to your special friends!

Imagine what a gift THAT would be to the people most special to you!

Dare to be exceptional.

Go for it.

Chapter One The Journey

Welcome aboard a journey toward.

Toward what, you ask?

Toward a different, perhaps better, more fulfilling, enlightened future. Toward a lighter, more empowered you.

Toward the life you were designed to create.

This journey will be full of surprises. There will be days of total breakthroughs followed by days of utter challenge -- and that's okay.

Breakthrough

Significant, noteworthy movement from point A to B, for whatever point A to B represents for you.

Some of you may ask yourself *"How long does this journey take; how can I accomplish what I want in the shortest length of time.*

In all reality, your journey has already begun just by beginning to read this book. The changes that will begin here will last you a lifetime; refining, creating, challenging new and old belief systems and creating-reinventing yourself daily.

> **Reinvention**
>
> *A departure from what came before or an embellishment of something that was in place, often even the most positive change represents upheaval.*

The techniques and exercises contained within these pages are nothing but a roadmap, a guide for a successful life change.

Not meant to show you an exact way to your destination but rather a purposeful view intended to open your eyes to the world you've created and provide a pathway to change.

What we can accomplish together in the next few days is whatever you make it. Some of you will set an ordinary goal. Some of you may make that goal; others won't.

Some of you will set your sights on becoming extraordinary. Some of you may make achieve greatness in the next 48 hours; others won't. My advice—

Dare something worthy.

You see, the effort to create is just that; effort. Small or large...doing something every day, creating a new reality, causing chaos in the old reality, to bring your dream within your grasp.

Our goal is the extraordinary, and that can be much more simplistic than you may think.

Still, consider this fact: in golf, 3 good shots out of 4 put you on par. That's 75/25, and that's all you need to make the journey a success.

Whether you create something mundane or reach for the sky is up to you. So choose your path well and hang on tight...it's a great ride called life.

Now, I won't lie to you – Climbing that mountain to the summit of your life can be one hell of a climb. Full of challenges and surprises.

But when you are climbing that mountain and hit those rough spots; take a moment and consider the alternative is to forever stay exactly where you are at right now and never wander beyond the confines of what you consider safe ground.

That safe ground is where most avalanches find their final home.

This is how life can manage to bury you -- by staying put.

Consider how fast life can snowball, and how much easier it is to hit a motionless target.

All of this is the result of fear.

And, as of today, you can dedicate yourself to living fearlessly.

Breakthrough to Success is written in a unique style that allows for direct answers and non-direct subconscious interaction. The goal is to get your conscious and your subconscious mind working on the day's challenges and lessons.

With that in mind, please understand that 'some' of the messages may not be so easy to understand at first.

That's okay...that's the way the course was designed.

Your mind will work overtime on the words as long as you read them and do the assignments. The end result is a program that teaches and alters negative patterns of thought at the same time.

Let's start today with the first of three

"Prepare Yourself to Breakthrough" exercises.

EXERCISE

Step one: stretch your legs.
Get up right now. It doesn't matter where you are -- you can do this anywhere. Inhale. Take a deep breath, and raise your arms above your head. Now, stretch.

People around you will assume you're just... stretching. You're not. You're reaching. Look up when you do this. See yourself in your mind's eye reaching for the next crevasse in a mountain; the next foot-hold. The next bit of level ground. The better view.

I'd like you to spend time just enjoying the little things.

Living in the moment.

This may sound trivial, perhaps even silly. Then again, most every simple answer confounds those seeking complication.

Let's return to having fun as we *grow* rather than merely *growing* old. Lesson number one for today is this:

Do not beat yourself up.

Please allow me to reiterate -- this big old mountain of life can be a heck of a climb.

You know it, I know it, and everyone who is already up there and waiting for you knows it. Those who have backslid and are now having to climb it again with a few injuries know it.

But, that's okay. Really. The key is to not beat yourself up any more than the climb itself does. That alone is enough to endure.

Hey, it's fun, but it's tough -- so don't feel the need to make it harder by weakening the only person making the journey.

You simply must stop harming our number one climber -- you. We need "you" for this endeavor. Having a depressed, nay-saying you will do us little good.

We need a you that is willing to forgive.

That's right -- I'm asking you to forgive yourself.

Right now.

Forgive your body for doing what your mind has asked it to do, or perhaps what your Map of Reality has told it to do. It's only trying to follow through.

For now, all I want you to do is say this...oddly enough, to your own body:

"Thank you for taking me this far. I realize you are only doing what you're told by my mind and my map of reality and I'm dedicated to learning what's really best for you in both areas. Let's work together from today on and breakthrough the limitations we've created."

Try it.

Forgiveness is massive. The sheer energy that fear, hate and anger generate is astounding, and that energy is like a huge magnet "pulling you down to earth."

Our goal is to climb above what we think our limitations are...to climb above our own mountain of doubt to find a larger world than we imagine. A greater world than we have dreamed. We cannot have this excess weight, so please -- cut it loose, right now. While you're at it, see what other excess weight you can cut loose before we start our journey.

See who else you can forgive.

Take this to the bank -- the journey to excellence begins with a clean mind, and forgiveness is the eternal cleanser.

EXERCISE

This exercise is twofold:

PART ONE:

Make a list of the three people you most want to influence during the next two days. Keep this list with you at all times. Under each name, write down how you want to influence them, and how committed you are to making your influence a reality.

What do you want them to see in you in the next two days? How do you want to see their lives impacted simply by seeing what you will accomplish?

Remember, you're making this journey for them as well as for yourself.

The larger you make your goal, the more important it becomes in your mind.

The more you focus on it, the more "urgent" it becomes... and your mind follows the call of the urgent.

PART TWO:

I would like you to have some 3-5-minute conversations sometime today with a few people. These are the people waiting for you, or perhaps with you in spirit -- the people you love the most.

Let them know that this step, this changing of reality is for you.

Let them know how your life will not be the same once you've seen the glimpse of the "possible."

Make sure they know you'll always be there for them, but demand the same in return.

Do not let anyone turn you away from the path you've decided to take -- the path toward abundance, health and personal mastery.

There are those who will want to tie you down. They are afraid of change, and they want you to keep them and their fear company. You cannot do that and care for them at the same time. Do not harbor anger toward them.

Remember, anger is energy that pulls you back to old realities. To be successful you must foster energy that "propels you forward". Only, always, and forever forward.

Instead, forgive and encourage them to join you. Most of the people you love the most will support you on your journey for excellence -- and that is a wonderful thing.

You need support. This journey is not to be made alone. You need support from those you "really want to influence."

That is the key.

Chapter Two   Values, Balance, Awareness

Many people have very a defined value system that is based upon their experiences and beliefs.

Many times these value systems were based on what they were taught in childhood.

Some of these values systems propel us into action and achieving our goals.

Others hold us back, keeping us stuck in arcane thinking or actions, trying to constantly prove that our Map of Reality is true.

So, what do values really mean?

Personal values and beliefs system are a ***"personal hallucination of reality"***; our human attempt of make sense of the world based upon what we perceive is right or wrong.

This next series of exercises will help define your current value and belief systems and allow you to see the inner message they bring.

So are you ready see exactly what your values and beliefs are?

Your answers may surprise you.

EXERCISE

Values

Review the list of 36 values. Prioritize them as you see that component within yourself by numbering them from 1 thru 36. Avoid using the same number twice.

TIP: *Be brutally honest. It's not how we "want" to be...it's how we actually are.*

Don't cheat yourself and read ahead. Do the work. Then turn the page.

3 **Honesty**

7 **Accountable**

26 **Financially secure**

15 **Compassionate**

25 **Independent**

2 **Risk Taker**

23 **Focused**

24 **Power**

8 **Goal Oriented**

19 **Leader**

9 **Organized**

1 **Aggressive**

10 **Persistent**

16 **Impulsive**

21 **Famous**

20 **Team Player**

6 **Safety**

14 **Meticulous**

5 **Integrity**

13 **Influential**

22 **Competitive**

4 **Persuasive**

11 **Articulate**

17 **Diverse**

12 **Fair**

18 **Confident**

Continue...

___Practical   ___Authoritative

___Free Spirit   ___Religious

___Flamboyant   ___Adaptable

___Trustworthy   ___Action-Oriented

___Tolerant   ___Successful

RESULTS

How to use the information from the Values exercise.

The top 12 components (1-12) define who you are right NOW.

The last 12 define who you are not.

The middle set (13-24) is the great self-saboteurs.

This is where you could have the most growth on your Breakthrough to Success.

EXERCISE

Balance

What does your balance sheet look like?

The categories given below will provide an overview of the major areas of your life. Use a 1-10 scale (with 10 being highest score) to rank your balance in these areas.

TIP: *Be brutally honest. It's not how we "want" to be...it's how we actually are.*

Keys Elements of a Balanced Life

Personal Health & Wellness *(in body, mind, spirit equally)*

1   2   ③   4   5   6   7   8   9   10

Spiritual *(inner harmony, living congruently with core values, relationship to Higher Power))*

1   2   ③   4   5   6   7   8   9   10

Relationships *(family, personal, professional, community)*

1   2   3   4   ⑤   6   7   8   9   10

Personal Development *(use of potential, self actualization)*

1   2   ③   4   5   6   7   8   9   10

> **Continue:**
>
> **Fun** *(rejuvenation, adventure, self expression, creativity)*
>
> 1   2   3   **(4)**   5   6   7   8   9   10
>
> **Financial Security** *(economically secure, adequate income from multiple sources)*
>
> **(1)**   2   3   4   5   6   7   8   9   10
>
> **Professional Development** *(recognition, achievement, accountability, advancement)*
>
> 1   **(2)**   3   4   5   6   7   8   9   10

Many times we become so busy putting out the fires in our lives we forget to stop and take a look at the condition of the forest we live in.

We go by day to day thinking the world is doing just fine then **BANG**, a tree drops on us.

Surprised?

You bet we are!

Everything was going along just perfect then out of left field came this.....

In reality the issues, problems and concerns were always there, we just got too busy to see them.

EXERCISE

Awareness

In this next exercise please list the **top 10 important things in your life.**

The things you can't live without.

Write them down in your notebook.

Here's just a few to stimulate your thinking.

Self Care	Family	Friends
Career	Fun	Children
Health	Sex	Fitness
Sleep	Intimacy	Money
Music	Dance	Sports
Food	Recreation	Quiet Time

Now, draw a circle.

Using the "pie chart" method, place each of the top 10 "important" items into the chart, the size of the slice representing the amount of time **_DAILY you actually do the activity_**. Write down the amount of time within the slice. Remember that there are only 24 hours in a day.

DO NOT REVIEW THE CHART AS YOU GO!

TIP: *Be brutally honest. It's not how we "want" to be...it's how we actually are.*

Now

Got **_EVERYTHING_** on your chart???

GOOD...you're done....

Time to review your chart and ask yourself some questions....

Is this the way you wish life to be?

Do you need to make changes or adjustments to your life chart?

Where can you make changes based upon your core values and beliefs i.e. the exercises you have just completed?

Have you forgotten anything that needs to be added to your chart?

Sometimes what we think that is important to us tends to take a backseat to life. We simply have GREAT intentions and plans but a lot of times day to day life gets in the way. Weight issues, health, finances, relationships, self improvement; we all know the drill.

The simple fact is that in the United States alone, there are enough self help, diet and life improvement books to reach the moon and back over ten times.

So the question is if there are that many ways, ideas and programs why aren't we all full of this knowledge? Why don't we all have the ideal body for us and are socially, emotionally and physically well balanced?

Life.

It gets in our way.

We get *SO* busy living that we forget to make a life.

We get so busy making a living, solving problems, putting our life fires that even though we may have the greatest of intentions we don't make time to do what is really important to us.

In fact most times we aren't even SURE of what is most important in our lives. We haven't taken the time or taught to fully understand that concept.

Oh we "think" we know…we "want to ***think*** we know"…ok, we "***hope***" we know…But how can we really be sure of what that "important" stuff is?

Do the next exercise. It just may surprise you….

EXERCISE

Importance

Note: In the last exercise I asked you to list the top ten things in your life. Please write down these top ten things once again. Do not read or go any further till you do this.

Now cross off five of these important items off your list. Do not read or go any further till you do this. Notice the emotions as you do this.

Now cross off one more. You will have four items of importance left.

Cross off one more. Three things that are the most important in your life is what you left. Again, notice the emotions.

Getting hard to choose isn't it?

Cross off one more. Two left.

Getting tough isn't it?

Now time to choose between the two remaining items.

Really hard now...having to choose between the two MOST important things in your life.....

Cross off one more.

The one that remains is the most important item, issue, event or thing in your life *at this particular time*.

Did your last item surprise you?

Now if your answer was anything besides the word YOU, only this question remains:

How much time do you dedicate to the most important thing in your life?

YOU!

Chapter Three   Release

Have you considered that the reason for 'any' dissatisfaction in your life may simply be due to the fact you didn't enjoy what you were doing?

What if you could teach yourself to enjoy anything that provided you with a greater view?

You see, we're all after a greater view:

- A world view that's sound and compassionate.
- A self-view that's compassionate and truthful.
- A future view that's truthful and progressive.
- A beautiful view of all the wonder around us.

Anything that propels you toward a greater view is something you can learn to enjoy.

Why?

Because we all love beauty. Start today with this thought:

Seek what is truly beautiful in life and to share it with everyone you love.

I'm not talking about "vanity" – although physical beauty is nothing to be ashamed of.

I'm speaking of true beauty – the beauty of a life in motion, of a person in growth, of a body in metamorphosis.

Become beauty.

Link beauty to your life. Remember, the view of life you seek is one of utter transcendence. One of awesome, breathtaking beauty.

To begin to change our current reality; the things that are holding us back from success, we must first begin by looking at the Mind.

We've already begun, you know – changing your focus from, *"I'm broke", "I'm a loser", "I'm ugly", or "I'm fat",* to *"I seek beauty in all things and will settle for nothing less."*

This is a major step forward. Your first step. Be excited about it – the first step is the hardest and yet one that anyone can make. Think about it.

Part of beauty is release. Beauty is the release of all things ugly and the pursuit of all things true.

Therefore, to be truthful with yourself, let's begin with one of the most powerful truth-based statements you can ever accept:

"I seek to release everything necessary to gain a beautiful view from any and all directions."

Perhaps you are glancing sideways and catch a glimpse of yourself in the mirror.

What do you see?

What do you need to **RELEASE** in order to see what you long for?

Do you need to release some fat?

How about some emotional baggage?

Unresolved issues from the past?

False perceptions about who are and what you can accomplish?

Some anger, perhaps?

How about expectations?

Can you see unrealistic expectations and the damage they've created in your eyes? Does this weigh you down?

Release it. Decide right now that you will release it, and you will do so without anger or remorse.

Be thankful for what these feelings and your body has taught you – and then kiss these feelings good-bye. Any physical challenges? Meet them with joy rather than anger.

You'll find your mind is much more open to coping and creative solutions when you are in a state of gratitude.

Everyone has something to release...

EVERYONE

EXERCISE

Releasing

Write out 5-10 things you will release over the next 2 days.

Don't worry about *"how"*.

Remember this: *"why"* is always more powerful than *"how"*.

Knowing *"why"* will propel you upward.

All the *"how's"* in the world can keep you stuck in neutral.

The answer never has been more knowledge.

The answer has always been a reason to act and act boldly.

Now that you have begun to release old outdated ideas, limiting beliefs and patterns, the next step is to begin loving yourself.

I mean truly being thankful for who you are...the good, the bad, the powerful, the weak...all your flaws and your strengths.

All of you.

Chapter Four   7 Steps to Loving Yourself and Others

> *Love is a state of <u>doing</u> and <u>being</u>.*
>
> *There are some very specific things to do in order to love either yourself or others. The <u>doing</u> is the same, the direction just changes.*

1)   GIVE. Start giving to yourself and others in as many ways as you can. Give physically, emotionally, intellectually, and intuitively. Do not worry about "getting"...just really develop your ability to give.

2)   RESPOND: Allow yourself the ability and the willingness to respond. Be responsible to yourself and then to others.

3)   RESPECT: Honor your emotions and the emotions of others who you want to love. Respect is not an issue of doing. It is an issue of honoring. So often when people try to gain respect from themselves or others, they look around for something to do. Then they work hard to doing whatever it is they decided would give them respect, only to discover that their respect level has not really changed. They feel like failures. To respect yourself is to honor your emotions. You honor your emotions by giving yourself the permission and safe space for the expression and release of what you honestly feel. To shed tears when they arise. To make laughter a part of daily living. To honor your inner child with play. To love and honor your feelings, and in doing so honor the feeling of others.

4) KNOW: There are two ways of knowing someone---through inflicting pain or through seeking understanding. Because so many are afraid to love, they inflict pain—one themselves and on others. Yes, one route of knowing is through pain, but there is another route. Seeking understanding begins with a conscious desire and concludes with a conscious commitment. It involves taking the time to really reach out—tenderly, to reach out...to develop the skill of loving, seeking understanding of yourself and others. You are not in this world to be understood, you are here to be understanding.

5) HAVE THE HUMILITY TO BE INTIMATE: Humility is the willingness to see each day as being brand new. It is the willingness to let people change instead of insisting that they never change. You create your reality primarily out of choice and belief. If you consistently choose to see people at their worst and believe that, then that is just the way they are. You WILL be right, but miserable. To be humble is to say, "That the way it's always been, AND it can be different now". Be humble enough to be close, tender and vulnerable with yourself and with those about whom you care.

6) HAVE THE COURAGE TO COMMIT: Commitment is really frightening to many of you. Fear of rejection and humiliation are the major culprits.

Fear of responsibility---*Can I handle it?* contributes massively to your refusal to be committed. To many, commitment feels like imprisonment. They confuse obligation with responsibility. When you consider committing yourself to another, often times your negative ego steps in with the question—*"If you can create it this good, couldn't you do better? Don't commit WAIT!"* It admonishes you not to commit, saying that something or someone better might show up. If something better DOES show up, you still wait. Commitment never comes. It takes courage to love.

7) CARE: Honestly care for yourself and how your life is going. Notice, this did NOT say, "Feel sorry for yourself". Love has nothing to do with self-pity. It said, "CARE". You don't need a reason to care. You ARE the reason. Just open your heart and your mind and begin. Let yourself care about others. Let yourself care about *yourself.*

There is more to it than this, though.

You do these seven steps in order to **accomplish something**.

It is the dynamic **between** these seven steps with the express purpose of providing the following that creates love.

The "In Between Steps"

SECURITY: Physical, emotional, intellectual and intuitive safety for yourself or for another. ***THIS*** is where love begins.

PLEASURE: To give, respond, respect or know yourself or someone else so as to provide them with short and long term pleasure---to be intimate, to be committed and to care for yourself or another so that you or they feel safe.

HONESTY & VULNERABILITY: To make it all right to let down the walls of defense. To let it be all right to be totally honest and open. To provide the space to expose your anxieties and doubts without fear.

TRUST: It is most powerful energy you can give yourself. It is also most precious and beautiful gift you can give to others.

REDUCED FEAR OF LOSS: If you had a dazzling piece of gold jewelry that you believed was just an inexpensive piece of alloy plated with gold, you would wear the ring anywhere and everywhere, doing everything without fear. Now you suddenly find out that the ring is NOT just plated, but PURE gold, a VERY rare gold at that, it is a priceless family heirloom and cannot be replaced. Suddenly you want to lock up the ring. You are afraid of wearing it anywhere. The fear of losing something so precious, so valuable is terrifying. When you love someone all fears evaporate, except one. The fear of loss is the only fear that increases as love increases. If you were to lose that love now, it could be devastating. If you love more, the value only increases and the fear of losing only increases. That is why many people run from love, of self or others. Ironically, the antidote to this fear of loss is to take a deep breath and love even more. That's right, the answer is to take a deep breath and give, respond, respect....and above all ***CARE***. For love to be more than simply a word, it should work at reducing the very fear it produces. So stop leaving the good china in the cupboard for use for special guests only. ***YOU ARE THAT SPECIAL GUEST!***

INTIMACY AND CARING: Act in such a way so as to create a resonance of closeness and tenderness, to create a resonance of freedom and safety. Become intimate with your own emotions, fears and dreams. Know without a shadow of doubt that you are worthy, are special and loved.

KNOWING: To communicate---to be empathetic. Let the other know that you know them. Let them know that you see their beauty AND the not-so-beautiful side, and you love them anyway. With self-love, admit your strength and love it. Admit your weakness and acknowledge it can be changed. Admit your ugliness, and love it. Quite so, it is easy to love beauty and the ugliness needs love too.

Always begin with yourself. Start with yourself in practicing your doing and being of love. Many of us are good at loving others but we forget ourselves in the mix. After practicing on yourself, then expand to include others, not just any others, but specific others, significant others. Once you have developed and refined your skills, once you are really good at loving, always intensify self love.

EXERCISE

Self Love

NOTE: You will need the following for this exercise:

paper (your Journal will work wonderfully)

black or blue pen and a red pen

You may be familiar with marriage vows. These are spoken vows of commitment and love to another person. The following exercises are a spoken vow of commitment and love for self. This may be extremely uncomfortable for some at first.

If so, just honor that, notice the emotions, let the tears flow and reframe them to **Yesterday I was...Today I am...**

The "VOID" exercise

During this next exercise when negative self talk or emotions rise, write them down in detail on paper with your black or blue pen. Then, with using your RED pen draw a line thru the negative statement write the word **VOID** across the negative statement and repeat **OUT LOUD**...

Yesterday I was ~~(VOID)~~

Today I am (positive statement)

Self Love

Remember....As you are looking yourself in the eyes, begin to notice the beauty instead of focusing on your flaws. Notice your emotions. When negative self talk or emotions arise, <u>write them down</u>, use the **VOID** exercise to reframe those thoughts.

Looking in the mirror, say, **"I love you"**.

Notice your emotions. When negative emotions arise, write them down, use the **VOID** exercise to reframe those thoughts.

Looking in the mirror, say, **"I respect you"**.

Notice your emotions. When negative emotions arise, write them down, use the **VOID** exercise to reframe those thoughts.

Looking in the mirror, say, **"I honor you"**.

Notice your emotions. When negative emotions arise, write them down, use the **VOID** exercise to reframe those thoughts.

After first doing this exercise, repeat the three phrases in every reflective surface you encounter. Notice your self-talk and the emotions and ***REFRAME THEM***!

I love you

I respect you

I honor you

Nine words that are so easy

Yet

Mean so very much

Chapter Five   Attraction and Creating

Imagine if you were able to put all of your past behind you so it didn't affect your future.

Who you were yesterday is gone...forgotten...there **IS NO PAST**...today was the first day of your life...Imagine your future is a blank canvas.

Who **would** you be?

Who **could** you be?

What **would** you do?

What **could** you do?

Hard to imagine isn't it?

Most of us have built barriers to keep ourselves from answers like those. Walls. Big thick strong Walls. Hurdles. Obstacles in the path to our success

I have two words for those.

Good.

Great.

Now we have something we can work with.

You see many of us dream, plan, think *what if, if only, when I*. We use positive affirmations and *attempt* to manifest success in our lives but in doing so we tend to forget one thing.

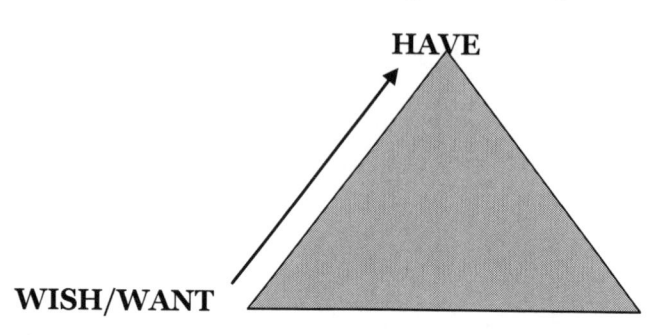

```
              HAVE
               ▲
              ╱│
             ╱ │
            ╱  │
           ╱   │
          ╱    │
         ╱     │
   WISH/WANT
```

This triangle represents unfulfilled plans; unrealized thinking, the typical *what if, if only, when I* mindset, positive affirmations and manifestations.

Guess what....it doesn't work. You may have noticed that there is a missing corner of this triangle.

So what is the missing piece? What **IS** the **GREAT SECRET**??

Folks, you got to ***DO*** something...that's right...it's called ***ACTION!***

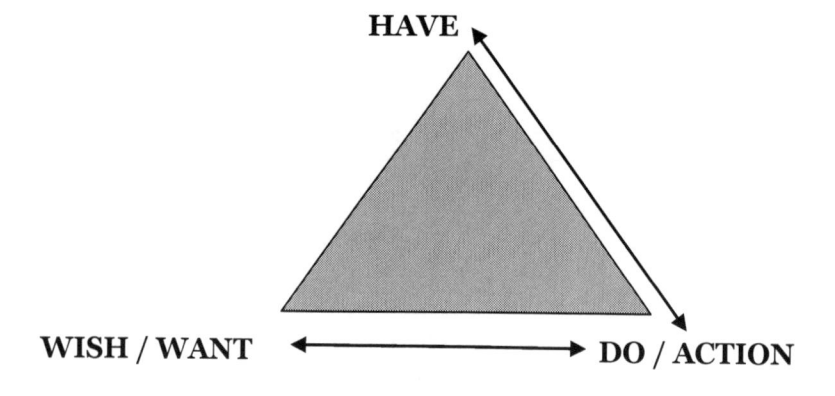

```
              HAVE
               ▲
              ╱ ╲
             ╱   ╲
            ╱     ╲
           ╱       ╲
          ╱         ╲
         ╱           ╲
   WISH / WANT  ◄──────►  DO / ACTION
```

~ 38 ~

Ultra Top Secret Success Formula:
Persistence + Action= Success

Ultra Top Secret??? Well. Maybe not but....It's simple right? Everybody knows that...

So why don't we **DO** it?

I know, you tried right to be successful?

You "tried" to do it right...You tried once, twice, three, twenty times.

Wrong.

Most of us "try" something a maximum of three times then give up. Really persistent ones maybe twenty at most...some are even heard to utter the immortal phrase *"It's just not meant to be"*.

B.S. That's just a great reason.

Flexibility requires persistence. Napoleon Hill summed it up all in one sentence:

"Persist until you succeed."

He told the story of Thomas Edison's ongoing series of failures in developing the light bulb. Edison was unbelievably flexible in the creation of the electric light bulb. When one strategy failed he utilized the next pathway then the next path until he attained his desired result. On his 784th attempt he could have said, *"You know it just wasn't meant to be."*

Had he done that maybe we wouldn't have electric light. But fortunately, it was meant to be because Edison saw it in his mind so clearly and had hundreds of alternate possibilities to make his intention manifest in reality.

Colonel Sanders, the finger lickin' chicken guy, traveled the country in a rumpled white suit, living in his car for **two years,** had doors slammed in his face and was refused **1009**, that's **ONE THOUSAND NINE** times before he heard his first *"Yes, I'll buy your recipe"*. Do the math on this one...that's almost **1.5 times per day for two years!!**

Ever hear of Walt Disney? Ol' Walt was turned down for financing of the "Happiest Place on Earth" ala **Disneyland** 302 times before someone gave him the money for creation of his dream.

I've never forgotten those stories and I've always used them as my motivator when I wanted to give up and offer the excuse, *"it just isn't meant to be."*

Here's the thing:

Everything you see around you was first a thought in the mind of someone who could have said, "Well, I guess it just wasn't meant to be."

Everything you see is the result of **Intention + Action.**

Everything.

The stumbling block is the "It just isn't meant to be right now."

And all this time you thought two, three, even twenty times was good enough....

Guess again:

Persistence + Action = Success

So why do we stop ourselves from achieving success?

Why do we do it?

Chapter Six   Map of Reality

In psychology there is a concept called Premature Cognitive Commitment or thinking.

What this means is that we tend to act out our lives out of automatic, habitual behaviors. Behaviors that we have done time and times again till we know longer consider what we are doing, we just do it. We make up our mind about our environment and the world around us based on the filters we have installed from childhood.

These filters are installed by our experiences. Our "truths". Or rather our hallucination of the truth, of reality.

You see; every day we watch the world and have experiences. What we tell ourselves about those experiences, what meanings we put upon them shapes our views. Imagine for a moment a big, five-gallon clear glass jar. Now fill that jar with 500 houseflies. Put a piece of clear plastic wrap over the mouth of the jar and shake it up. No worries, there is approx 48 hours of air in the jar for the flies.

The flies will begin buzzing around the jar, banging into the sides, the bottom and top. They can see the outside world; they know that it is there but they can't get to it. As they bang against the jar they begin to distort their view of the world they knew and begin making cognitive decisions and self-limitations about their environment. When the plastic wrap is removed 48 hours later, when the jar is open, 99.9% of the flies, 499 of them will stay in the jar.

Why?

Because they have made cognitive commitments and self-limiting thoughts about their environment. They simply decided it couldn't/ wouldn't happen, and so it became truth to them.

Sound familiar?

This is the very same thing we tend to do to ourselves. What this teaches us is that we have made decisions, estimates and decided what we can and cannot do based on our life experiences and what people have told us that we believed. Even more profound is that we have made those estimates and limiting decisions based on what we have paid attention too!

Just like the flies in the jar we have made decisions about who we are and limited our capabilities based on the filters we have installed. We continue to act out those beliefs even when the proverbial plastic wrap is taken off our jar. Just like those flies we have created our map of reality. Our internal representation of self.

As humans, these ideas of self form our opinions our belief systems and views of the world around us. And while those values and belief systems made have been useful at one time, just like the plastic wrap was once true for the flies, those beliefs may not be true today.

So how DID those belief systems get in there? Human beings are conceptualizers, storytellers, and thinkers. Our main communication medium is language. We are meaning making machines. We have to place our stamp, our version or hallucination of reality on everything that enters our minds. We have to have a meaning i.e., our interpretation of the event, in order to process the information so our minds can then take the appropriate actions.

We all begin constructing a story about life and our relationship to it almost from the moment we are born. In a sense, each of us not only has a story but also is the story. We write our life script, our movie, in which we are the main character. We are the heroes. We get to choose the scenes, setting and appropriate music for our theme song. Things happen to us. Some good things, some bad things. We take actions. We witness events and outcomes. We make decisions, some good ones and some bad ones. We have good guys and bad guys. We draw conclusions. And then we weave it all into an ongoing, always consistent, never ending narrative tapestry based upon our unique hallucination of reality around us.

The main theme of our story, our life script, is our sense of self; who we are or better yet, who we believe we are. Our life script and who we become is heavily influenced by what we were told when we were young and what we chose to believe about ourselves at that time.

Were we told that we were smart or stupid? Lazy or hardworking? Are our siblings really better than us? Are we beautiful, handsome or homely? Are we destined to be rich or poor? Are we supposed to act the role of the victim or the hero? Are we part of an elite group or a persecuted minority? A good person or a bad person? A winner or a loser?

When we were offered each of these views, which of these scenarios did we believe about ourselves at the time, accept them as truth and allowed them to be embedded in our young subconscious minds and become reality for us when we grew older? When we were children, our world was typically very small; it consisted mainly of our parents, teachers and other grownups that we automatically labeled as the authorities on this exciting new world we were born into. We were positive they knew what they are talking about. They had to know everything. They had seen it all we thought, they had been there, done that and their words must be right.

In this picture, it is only natural that we designed our stories, our scripts, about ourselves based on the definitions, examples and influences that our parents, our teachers and those other authority figures that we knew were right had given us. They provided our basis for our imagined strengths and weaknesses, whether or not those definitions were in our own best interests.

To better understand the impact of critical language on children, it is vital to understand that children hear and process language differently from adults. They take things said more literally than adults and tend to believe without question, especially when those ideas and statements come from an authority figure. When we were young children we didn't particularly have the intellectual maturity to question our evaluation of our parents, to let their words roll of us like water on a ducks back.

Example; we are 3-years-old and just spilled orange juice all over our clothes at breakfast and our stressed out, late for work parents yelled, "Can't you drink that without making a mess of yourself?"

Typically we didn't think: "You know, I think my parents have too high expectations of me. They have placed upon me very unrealistic goals for the short time I've been on earth. I am only 3-years-old. As a matter of fact, I would say that the majority of my fellow nursery school friends come to school with some portion of their breakfast on their shirt. So I am not going to let this bother me!" Well, at least, most of us didn't anyway.

As children we accepted their evaluation of us. We didn't ask questions, we just obeyed. If they said we couldn't drink without making a mess, we must become that mess. Ironically, when we become our parents' negative projection it is a form of "honoring our parents." A "good" child listens to what their parent tells them and accepts it as truth, often literally and we are pre-programmed by our parents, teachers and other authority figures to be "good" children.

When the grownup in our life says, "You are stupid," we accept that we are stupid. When they ask why we "can't do anything right," we accept our incompetence as a "true-ism". When we are told that we are a "bad boy" or "bad girl" naturally we assume this must be true. We might even try harder to be good. But all the while we know deep inside in our hearts that we must be bad. After all, mother or father knows best, don't they?

Children haven't yet developed the critical faculty that allows adults to evaluate new information, rejecting or accepting it based on our past experience. They simply haven't accumulated the experiences and definitions to base those decisions on yet. Children are listening and watching forming their little pictures of whom they are and how life is. And they generally believe what they are told literally, whether that picture is positive or negative.

How else could we convince them that a fat old man with a snow white beard, wearing a red velvet suit, riding in a sleigh pulled by flying reindeer, will come down their chimney (even if there ISN'T one) with a bag of presents just for them every December 25th, but only if they behave themselves the entire rest of the year? Wow, I'd love to meet the parent that came up with THAT story to make their kids behave.

Personal Map of the World

We become products of our personal map of the world. Our skewed view of reality. Our hallucination of the truth.

If you continue to think and act in the same way; you'll get the same results. You MUST begin to change your thinking in order to change your reality.

"Historical truth" is immaterial. Since everything is true to the person believing it, evaluating whether its right or wrong becomes a moot point. If YOU believe it, it's true. What you FOCUS on becomes your truth.

Now toss into the mix our constant need to be "right". That's right; we all have a need to affirm that we are right. What this means is that if we have a belief that we are a loser, that we "can't" do something; we WILL be right. We will create situations that will MAKE us right. We will deliberately self-sabotage ourselves in the name of being right. We will distort reality, attract a negative and then act on that negative....just to be right.

So how can we change?

Since the subconscious mind processes information at 1-10 million bytes of information or thoughts per second and we can only *"hold onto"* seven (plus or minus 2) of those thoughts, it's imperative that we learn how to choose which thoughts we hold onto. We do this by changing focus.

So why are you choosing your current reality?

You may be telling yourself that there is NO way in hell that you are choosing to being stuck in your present life and not achieving your goals and dreams.

But take a moment and re-examine that belief:

Is there any time that you begin to doubt yourself?

Any time you begin to question worthiness?

Any time you begin to question your abilities?

You may be stuck because you are DAMN good at focusing. Only trouble is; you are focusing on the "cant's" instead of the "can's".

By allowing yourself to doubt or change focus to negative you are getting what you want.

And that is to be right!

Do you think of *possible* or *impossible*?

Chances are you're presently thinking in the impossible. That is to say that you may have told yourself you can but there is still a nagging doubt and you are retreating to "safe" ground. What you have already always known. Remember when you were writing down those dreams and asking yourself why? Was there a little voice that said "because"?

Instead of asking what's wrong, ask what's right! Focus on possibility instead of the impossible. We'll get to the impossible soon enough.

Toss out the rulebook about what you "have" to do… Because when you focus on what you HAVE to do, you're not focusing on what you WANT to do.

Here's my suggestion:

Quit focusing on making a living and

begin focusing on making your life.

"Have to" changes focus from possibility and moves it into impossibility.

Young children are taught to play games with each other. Author Robert Fulghum taught us in his great book, *"Everything I Wanted To Know I Learned in Kindergarten"* to play nice, share and take naps every day. Children play games every day and are taught that they may win, or they may lose but never, never, EVER QUIT! People grow up learning that they must play, struggle, compete, and finally win or lose. Since there can only be one winner in a game, most of us learn to lose. Learn to do things that we don't want to do but do anyway, because "it's the right way to play the game". But to quit just to quit is unthinkable.

So what happens if we "quit"? If you quit doing something that you perceive you must do, you may just find out that you didn't have to do IT at all?

Because most of us think we know what we want from life, and we may even have a bit of an idea what is stopping us or at the very least we know whom we can blame.... *(Boy THAT one is sure a convenient excuse for failure isn't it? "It's not MY fault; it's because of my <u>fill in the blank</u>.)*

But the first step in changing our lives to become who we want to be is accepting what has happened in our past...we aren't and can't change what has happened.

That's a Kodak moment. But realizing that it *IS* the past *NOT* the future and taking responsibility of who and what we are today. Not who we will be tomorrow because tomorrow we will be someone different.

Taking responsibility for our actions *today*.

Right now.

Putting the past IN the past where it belongs and letting go of it controlling our decisions about the future.

Also few have ever really looked into all that we can be. Few of us have ever learned how to dream.

Today we start down the path to change the way we think...start to remove those barriers and walls.

Ok so now that we know that positive affirmation, simple manifestation and all that other stuff doesn't work...so what does?

Questions:

Asking a question that you don't have the answer to jumpstarts a portion of your brain called the Reticular Activating System in search of that answer.

The really cool part of the RAS is that it will keep coming up with ideas and suggestions till one of them works!

The Reticular Activating System is the **attention center** in the brain. It is the key to "turning on your brain," and seems to be the center of motivation. The RAS is connected at its base to the spinal cord where it receives information projected directly from the ascending sensory tracts. The brain stem reticular formation runs all the way up to the mid brain. As a result, the RAS is a very complex collection of neurons, which serve as a point of convergence for signals from the external world and from interior environment. In other words, it is the part of your brain where the world outside of you, and your thoughts and feelings from "inside" of you, meet.

Let's put this into plain language:

Imagine your brain as a blank computer, no programs, and no data. The RAS (reticular activating system) would be the software code programmer. Whatever you wanted your computer to do would have to be programmed in. Negative thoughts, stopping words that came out of your mouth such as "I can't" etc would program exactly that into your mind and that's how you would operate. It's the "garbage in, garbage out" principle. Perhaps you can begin to see how important what kind of programming, i.e. thoughts or language that enters your brain is.

Imagine what would happen if you became extremely aware of the words coming out of your mouth? Every time you caught yourself saying something negative you began to reframe that thought with a positive sentence?

"I don't know if I can do that…" would become, **"Yesterday, I don't know if I could have done that but today I know I can…"** **Positive reframing** begins the reprogramming process…

Language is much more than simple words.

Before the words can come from your mouth they must first be a thought in the brain.

Now…imagine that…you must **THINK** about what you say before you say it…

I'm a very big proponent of action, labor and discipline. In fact I devoted one of the five major pieces to the life puzzle to the subject of action and labor. But now let me add another key word to the labor equation - **skillful**. Yes, *skillful action and labor*.

We need the skills to help build our family's dreams, the skills to stir up an enterprise and make it successful. We need skills to build equities for the future. We need skills of all kinds.

How about this - skillful language.

If you just talk to your family you can hold them all together; but if you skillfully talk to your children you can help them build dreams for the future. That is why I spend so much time on communication - how to affect others with words. You can't be lazy in language - it costs too much. What if you meant to say *"what's troubling you?"* and instead you said *"what's wrong with you?"* Wow, now that's too big a mistake to make in communication isn't it? Look at the pictures you just created….

And sure you could have made that mistake 10 years ago, maybe even 10 DAYS ago but not now. Simply by reading this book, doing the exercises you should have begun to get much more aware of the power of words and mind pictures than before you started.

Skills multiply labors by two, by five, by ten, by fifty, by one hundred times.

Here's great example courtesy of John Rohn:

You can chop a tree down with a hammer but it takes about 30 days, that's called labor. But if you trade the hammer in for an ax, you can chop the tree down in about 30 minutes. What's the difference in 30 days and 30 minutes?

Skills.

Skills made the difference.

So do what you can – take action and labor.

But also do the best that you can do – work with improved skills.

You will find that the actions/labor combined with new skills will start producing something amazing called miracles.

Miracles with your money, miracles with your family and miracles in every part of your life.

Your next exercise is to become **VERY** skilled in the use of your language.

Listen for any negative statements or thoughts coming from within.

Catch yourself.

Then reframe that thought using something like "**Yesterday I was_____but today I am_____**"

Eliminate negative words such as **try, can't, should, would, couldn't, etc.**

Use the word **CHOOSE** instead!

I **CHOOSE** to eat better; I **CHOOSE** to be more successful.

Catch negative thoughts and reframe those.

If someone should use negative language around you, about you etc, pause, then reframe his or her statement.

REFRAME THE FOCUS

EXERCISE

This exercise is to get a journal.

Don't use a simple lined tablet for this, honor yourself with a real, honest to goodness, **VERRY** cool journal. Don't use an old one that you started for something else, get a new journal.

A **SUCCESS** Journal.

Here's the difference between success and failure.

Write down on the first page of your new journal:

Success: *A few simple disciplines practiced every day*
Failure: *A few errors in judgment repeated every day*

The difference between someone that is successful

and someone that is not is

simply the quality of their questions.

EXERCISE

Dreams

Now it's time to get you dreaming of the things that haven't even entered your mind yet that are all possible. It's time to teach you how to **dream...**not the kind that you have at night but dreams that create possibilities.

Just take a moment and look around wherever you are right now. Everything around you, no matter where you are, it all started with a thought, a dream.

A dream is just a reality that hasn't been created yet. So here my friend is where we begin to create the reality of the new you.

In your success journal using these **_three guidelines_** write down whatever comes to your mind. Your thoughts, your dreams, your possibilities....

The serious, the wild, the realistic, the crazy, the local, the global, the totally over the top, insane, it could never happen to me kind of dreams.

Don't censor them or even **READ** them... just write them.

Here are the three questions or guidelines to get you started.

Think about them, and then let your mind run wild.

Write down as many as you can.

Start with this list:

#1) *If Failure wasn't an option, if success was guaranteed; what would you do with your life? What could you do?*

#2) *If there was no fear; what would you do with your life? What could you do?*

Add these to your list...

#3) *If money was no object or obstacle; what would you do with your life? What could you do?*

Now add these to your list...

Ok...So WHY are you still reading????

What are you waiting for?

START WRITING!

Good Job! Now onto the NEXT exercise...

EXERCISE

Focus

#1) Circle and write down one of your dreams. The top one. Number 1. Now write down your intent for that dream. Now write down 4 things about that dream that you can put into action this week! ***AND THEN DO THEM!!!*** Focus intent with action. Don't think small, think large. If you begin to think small, you act small and will attract small. Focus with intent to be large, to be successful and to do it with ease. Record each day what you did and how it felt. Record ALL emotions.

#2) Create a focus plan. The focus plan is one thing to do each day that brings you closer to your goal. Whether eliminating self-talk, changing focus or physical effort, it's all action.
A focus plan is:

What you want

Why you want it

What you need to get it

What actions you are taking every day toward that goal

Notice any voices that are speaking to you, ones attempting to stop you. When you begin to hear these, **CHANGE YOUR FOCUS TO THE POSSIBLE!**

Here's the success formula:

- Focus in what you are brilliant at to achieve your goals, dreams and create wealth. Each and every minute of the day you decide your intentions. Make them positive ones!

- Record and document those actions and emotions.

- Stay away from and / or eliminate toxic people from your life. What you surround yourself with influences you greatly.

- Stop negative self-talk. **CHANGE THE FOCUS**

- Talk and think about what is **right** not what is **wrong**.

- Based on the answers that you gave on the belief questionnaire you were given at the beginning of this book, review where you want your life to be in six months.

Now…As you look in the mirror in the morning; ask yourself three questions about what it would take to get there. Write them down.

Three different questions every evening. Write those down.

A total of six questions every day.

Each and every day will be new questions.

Never repeat the same question.

Don't worry about the answers for now, just ask yourself the questions. Let the little reticular guy earn his keep. The questions that you begin to ask yourself begin to program a new reality.

Time to get ready for the answers....

Chapter Seven   Creating New Reality

> **There are only two main realities in life:**
>
> ***Reasons*** **(excuses) or** ***Results*** **(action).**
>
> **If you aren't getting the *Results* you want...**
>
> **It's because you've got great *Reasons***

It's the choice which one will become the all-powerful and the ruling factor in our lives. The choice of which path we choose to follow and live out our days on earth. The choice of the taking responsibility and determining for ourselves the quality of our lives. We **<u>CAN</u>** choose success and happiness.

Or we can choose to blame others, our parents, teachers, bosses, the general public, the media, the government, the man on the moon etc., was mean, hurt us, the world has never given us a break, life generally sucks and that's why we are stuck like we are…I guess I'll go eat worms…..

But is this really true? Or are we giving ourselves the gift of the perfect excuse for failing? For accepting defeat? For not being persistent until we succeed?

Did you know that it takes ***just as much planning to fail as it does to succeed?***

I've heard that a definition of insanity is banging your head repeatedly against a wall expecting a different feeling each time.

That's not what I'm suggesting.

The fact is, I was really good at this head banging, feeling sorry for myself, can't do it, not good enough stuff for quite a long time until I made the **decision** to give it up.

That's what it takes to make a change.

A decision and commitment.

Making the attempt, looking at what went right, what went wrong, adjusting, making changes, making the attempt time after time, and persisting till success happens.

I am asking you to make a decision.

Making a decision and holding yourself accountable will change your life.

Yesterday is gone. Tomorrow is nothing but possibility. Possibility of becoming anyone and doing anything you want. But you have to decide. You are going into battle for the rest of your life. This is a battle that you will win. Not because or for anyone else.

This one is for you.

I've also been told to draw that battle line in the sand. Well that may work for some...but for **REAL GUARANTEED** success, sand just isn't permanent enough. Draw this line in cement. My suggestion is making that the first step.

Draw your line in the cement.

Begin giving up the *reason* and begin working on the *result.*

It worked for me, it *will* work for you.

Make the decision. Make the commitment to yourself.

You deserve it.

EXERCISE

Reasons VS Results

Note: You will need a black or blue ink pen and a red pen ink pen for this exercise. Do NOT continue till you get these items.

Using the black or blue ink pen, look at your dreams that you have written down and circle your top three. These should be the dreams that really interest you. At least one of these should be fairly attainable in the future. In other words, no **"King of the World"** stuff....

Now write down the first dream that you circled and ask yourself this next question out loud. In your mind you will hear a small voice reply with an answer.

Write down the first reply or feeling that you get...Don't think about or contemplate the answer, just write down what you feel, hear, sense.......

Question: (Out Loud) ***So why haven't you done it?***

Repeat this for every dream that you have circled using the same pen.

Now go back to the first dream that you circled and wrote down the negative feedback too.

Using the **red ink pen**; draw a line through that negative statement and write the word ***VOID*** across the negative statement. As you write the word, say the following statement out loud,

"That was yesterday, not tomorrow"

Ready???

Let's go on to the next exercise

EXERCISE

Action Questions

Now using your top three dreams or goals you can also begin to reframe your daily questions, adding them to the mix.

How can I make this happen?

What would it take to do _____?

How soon could I begin to_____?

Write these questions down also.

Be aware of any feelings as you write...you may just want to jot those down as well...

There are no right or wrong answers to these exercises, no grades either.

That's not what this book is all about.

It's about life.

Your life.

What you want to do, what you want to become and where you want to take that life.

Reasons or Results...

You have the

Power to make the Choice.

Chapter Eight   Easy

Before we start this chapter, I want you to take a few moments and reflect on the previous chapters and the work you have done so far, what changes have taken place...and yes, ask yourself a few simple questions...

Where was I before starting this journey?

What changes have happened in my life?

What changes have happened in my thoughts about myself?

What changes have happened in my thoughts about my abilities?

With changes happening at such a rapid pace, sometimes we need to slow down and remember what we find important and what purpose we will serve in this lifetime.

And if the pace isn't as fast as you would like it to be, don't get discouraged. You are **EXACTLY** where you need to be at this time.

There is an old Buddhist saying that goes:

Release all expectations of the result.

This is where you want to be, releasing expectation and allowing the universe to do its job.

That doesn't by any means we can't help things along and take action towards our goals and dreams but simply release your expectations of how *fast* things **should** happen. They will happen at their own speed...exactly when you are ready for it...just put it out there...then take action...the Universe hears you...

"If your next step doesn't scare you...take a bigger one"

Anonymous

A lot of times we humans HAVE to do things the HARD way...because we have been taught (VERY well most times) that there are no easy ways to life.

Take a moment and think of all the metaphors for easy living that you have been taught while growing up.

My life motto is just the opposite...

I've done the hard way...it sucks...the easy way is **MUCH** better...now remember *"Easy"* does not mean cheap, sliding by or an excuse to slack off...all it means is that by thinking, acting and most of all **LIVING** with the new mindset that life, work, relationships etc CAN be easy we are beginning to reframe our minds to that new reality and make it come true.

The **Simple** way is most often the best way so here are some simple rules to live by...

The following is a brilliant excerpt from the "Four Agreements" by Don Miguel Ruiz

BE IMPECCABLE WITH YOUR WORDS

Speak with integrity. Say only what you mean. Avoid using the spoken word to speak against yourself or to gossip about others. Use the power of your words in the direction of truth and love.

DON'T TAKE ANYTHING PERSONALLY

Nothing others do is because of you. What others say and do is a projection of **their own reality, their own dream**. When you are immune to the opinions and actions of others, you won't be the victim of needless suffering.

DON'T MAKE ASSUMPTIONS

Find the courage to ask questions and express what you really want. Communicate with others as clearly as you can to avoid misunderstandings, sadness and drama. With just this one agreement, you can completely transform your life.

ALWAYS DO YOUR BEST

Your best is going to change from moment to moment; it will be different when you are healthy opposed to being sick. Under any circumstance, simply do your best and you will avoid self-judgment, self-abuse and regret.

Remember...it CAN be EASY...

Chapter Nine　　　　Money

Ok...now let's talk about money.

Yes, the OTHER talk our parents never got right...

No, I'm not talking about lack of money, wishing for money, dreaming of money or even the kind of money that grows on trees... but actual ***intentional*** steps ***YOU*** can take to make and attract more money to you.

And if you are like most people in order to bring more money into your life we may need to change a few beliefs about that green piece of currency we call ***MONEY***!

My friends, we have been taught about money through the media, our parents, our grandparents etc and most of what we have been taught is through stories, experiences and most of that has been negative.

So most of us need to change some belief systems if we are going to be successful in the money field.

The first belief that we need to change is that we ***NEED*** to be poor to learn something.

Well my friends, I think I've learned enough of THAT lesson.

> **"I have been poor and I have been rich...
> Rich is better"**
>
> **~Sophie Tucker~**

So let's all **CHANGE** that belief; that you need to be poor to learn a lesson...that you aren't worthy of being rich...you're not deserving.

Reframe that statement and the belief right now...

It's not a crime to be rich nor a virtue to be poor...

But Ron... I already know I **AM** deserving...

Really???

OK...let's do a simple test.

EXERCISE

Money

Here are some common beliefs or messages about money.

Say each one out loud and notice how it makes you feel.

Write down your thoughts in your journal. Which ones ring true to you?

Which ones were you raised with? Which do you live by and which do you reject?

What other adages come to you as you say them?

If it is a lack or negative thought, take out your red ink pen and remember to write the word **VOID** across it then using the *"That was Yesterday"* statement reframe that thought into a positive.

A bird in the hand is worth two in the bush.

A fool and his money are soon parted.

A penny saved is a penny earned.

All work and no play make Jack a dull boy.

Daddy will always take care of you.

Diamonds are a girl's best friend.

Don't count your chickens before they hatch.

Don't look a gift horse in the mouth.

Don't put your eggs all in one basket.

Hard work always leads to success- the harder you work, the luckier you get.

Marry for love, not for money.

It's just as easy to fall in love with a rich man as a poor one.

Money doesn't grow on trees.

Money is the root of all evil.

Money is a sign of success.

Money can't buy happiness.

Money isn't everything.

Money makes the world go round.

Time is money.

You can never be too rich or too thin.

You only get what you pay for.

Interesting where you went, isn't it?

The dollar bill, whether or not it's a 10, 20, 50 or 100-dollar bill is simply energy. If you begin to think of money as energy it takes on a different form.

I'm reminded of a story I once heard about a man that saved every nickel he made. He was mean hearted and the world around him reacted to him in a negative way. His name was Scrooge. I'm sure that you have heard the story and remember the ending. Scrooge found out that hoarding his wealth made him a lonely bitter man but when he gave from his heart the universe rewarded him tenfold, both in love from his fellow man and increased wealth.

Most of us think the best way to have more money is to hoard it.

But sadly, that's not the case. Can you hoard energy? Or does it increase when you give it away?

How many of you have given a dollar to a homeless person on the side of the road holding a sign? How many of you have looked the other way?

By holding onto that dollar you are essentially telling the universe that you cannot "afford" to help someone. That you are not abundant in your life.

So here's what I want you to do sometime this week.

Do it today if possible.

If not today, as soon as possible; yes I know what I am asking you to do sounds completely ridiculous but **JUST DO IT**.....you'll never regret the lesson and feeling.

Take a $20 dollar bill, go to the bank and get 20 one-dollar bills. Keep these in your pocket.

Not your purse, not your wallet...your **POCKET.**

Each day find a ***creative way*** to give away one dollar.

Not only to someone that needs it but to someone that ***doesn't*** need it.

Someone prosperous. A complete stranger.

No talking, no conversation or no explanation other than ***"Here, this is for you",*** and walk away.

Do not look back...just allow yourself to feel good about doing something good for someone else.

This teaches you to give with a generous heart and that there will always be more money coming to you. You are beginning to live from a space of abundance instead of a place of lack belief.

Here is a true story about a way that the native hunters in Africa and how they catch monkeys:

The hunters know that if they leave a nut in a hole of a tree, the nut being slightly smaller than the hole itself the monkeys will find it.

When the monkeys find the nut they will grab hold of it and try to bring it out from the hole. But in making a fist to hold onto the nut, their paw will not pass back through the hole in the tree. The monkey will not let go of the nut because they cannot grasp the idea that there could be more nuts elsewhere and they MUST hang onto THIS nut and the hunter can easily capture the monkey.

The monkey believes there is no more nuts to be found and must hold onto the one he has. Just like we may try to hold onto money, living in a lack or negative space instead of circulating it and living abundantly.

EXERCISE

What would you do?

Note: I suggest that you take your time to think about, meditate or use self-hypnosis on the following scenarios then write your responses. Notice any lack or negative beliefs that surface and **DO NOT** allow them to be your editor.

Fully Abundant:

You have all the $$ you need now and in the future.

Money is now longer a limitation of any kind.

What will you do now?

How will you live your life from this moment forward?

Limited Time:

You have just learned that a disease will end your life suddenly within five to ten years.

There is no cure for the disease, and no uncomfortable symptoms- just sudden death.

How will you change your life knowing that you will die sooner than you thought?

What will you do in the limited and uncertain time you have left?

One Year to Live:

A medical advancement has allowed your diagnosis to be accurately pinpointed to one year left of life.

How will you live your last year?

24 Hours:

You learn today, in your present circumstances of life that you have 24 hours to live.

What regrets do you have?

What longings?

What unfulfilled dreams are you aware of?

What do you wish you had done, said, been, and completed?

EXERCISE

Your Money Autobiography

Please spend approx. 1 hour or so writing this assignment. You will discover that this is a VERY powerful tool for understanding the roots of your present beliefs, choices and behaviors concerning money. You will come to understand the money myths and messages you grew up with and how they perpetuate your current money patterns. Use the questions as guidelines to help you focus on the feelings as much as the factual information. Your money autobiography will provide you with a wealth of information.

Money in your early life.

What role did $$$ play in your childhood?

What are your three earliest memories of $$$?

What messages about $$$ did you receive from your father, your mother?

What were the family stories about $$$? i.e. Uncle Fred losing his business, Aunt Sally marrying rich etc and were these stories told with admiration or disapproval?

What is your first memory involving $$$ and a close relative, a shopkeeper, a neighbor, a peer?

Describe a childhood experience about $$$ that has stuck with you and how it may have affected your current $$$ beliefs and behavior?

Did you ever worry about $$$ as a child? And in what form did your worry take?

When did you first become aware that your family was richer than some and poorer than others? And what feeling came with this awareness?

Was scarcity or abundance the tone of your household?

Was there a rich or poor relative or branch of the family?

How did $$$ come to you as a child- an allowance, stealing or gifts?

What was your first earning experience?

As a teen did you agree with or rebel against your parents and families attitude about $$$?

Did you ever make a vow about $$$ when growing up- (example- I'll never go hungry again) and how is that vow alive in your life today?

How have your beliefs about $$$ hurt your life or caused you suffering?

Do you continue to make choices based on your early money imprinting?

Make a list and in doing so look how you feel when you:

- Pay bills
- Are asked for a charitable contribution
- Apply for a loan
- Are asked for a loan
- Shop for groceries
- Shop for clothes
- Shop for new glasses
- Split a restaurant check
- Pick up the tab at a restaurant
- See advertisements for luxury cars
- Homes and vacations etc
- Shop for a car
- Hear what others have in retirement accounts
- Set the rates for your services or accept a designated wage.

Do you want to continue to live by these messages?

Now that you have completed the above exercise, look back on your answers that you have written.

Where did those thoughts and ideas begin?

What changes do you want to make?

How do you WANT to feel about the questions and scenarios?

Using the new tools that you have been taught what focus plan could you develop and use to take action to instill your new beliefs and make them reality?

OK...you made it...

At least to the last exercise...

So are we done yet?

Not quite....

You see...in all reality...you've just begun

You have the rest of your life to live...

Chapter Ten — Review Your Changes

FINAL EXERCISE

Since the beginning of this book there has been a common theme.

One of creating a new reality for yourself by developing a new belief that you indeed DO possess the power to create a brand new world no matter what the circumstances of your present situation is.

You do indeed have all you need right at your fingertips.

You always have.

I'm reminding of a movie called the Wizard of Oz...

In this movie a young girl named Dorothy asks for the power to go home and by the final scene discovers that all though her experiences she always had the power to change...she just didn't know how. All she had to do is click her heels three times and life could change.

Well, you may not have ruby slippers but all you need is the courage to step out of the limiting beliefs and allow your true self to shine through.

Already many changes have happened to you simply by listening to the enclosed , reading, absorbing and doing the exercises in this book.

Here's a great way to see just how much you've changed.....

Remember the Values and Balance exercises at the beginning of the book?

Here they are again...

Do the exercises...then compare them with the first set.

See the changes...

No peeking now...

Then do the last exercise...

This is the beginning of the new reality you have been building all throughout this book.

Writing your new life script...designing the new you...

The one where anything is possible...

Welcome to the new you....

Reach for the stars

Dare something worthy...

you *CAN* do it.

EXERCISE

Values

Review the list of 36 values. Prioritize them as you see that component within yourself by numbering them from 1 thru 36. Avoid using the same number twice.

TIP: *Be brutally honest. It's not how we "want" to be...it's how we actually are.*

Don't cheat yourself and read ahead. Do the work. Then turn the page.

___ Honesty   ___ Impulsive

___ Accountable   ___ Famous

___ Financially secure   ___ Team Player

___ Compassionate   ___ Safety

___ Independent   ___ Meticulous

___ Risk Taker   ___ Integrity

___ Focused   ___ Influential

___ Power   ___ Competitive

___ Goal Oriented   ___ Persuasive

___ Leader   ___ Articulate

___ Organized   ___ Diverse

___ Aggressive   ___ Fair

___ Persistent   ___ Confident

Continue...

___Practical   ___Authoritative

___Free Spirit   ___Religious

___Flamboyant   ___Adaptable

___Trustworthy   ___Action-Oriented

___Tolerant   ___Successful

EXERCISE

Balance

What does your balance sheet look like?

The categories given below will provide an overview of the major areas of your life. Use a 1-10 scale (with 10 being highest score) to rank your balance in these areas.

TIP: *Be brutally honest. It's not how we "want" to be...it's how we actually are.*

Keys Elements of a Balanced Life

Personal Health & Wellness *(in body, mind, spirit equally)*

1   2   3   4   5   6   7   8   9   10

Spiritual *(inner harmony, living congruently with core values, relationship to Higher Power))*

1   2   3   4   5   6   7   8   9   10

Relationships *(family, personal, professional, community)*

1   2   3   4   5   6   7   8   9   10

Personal Development *(use of potential, self actualization)*

1   2   3   4   5   6   7   8   9   10

Continue:

Fun *(rejuvenation, adventure, self expression, creativity)*

1   2   3   4   5   6   7   8   9   10

Financial Security *(economically secure, adequate income from multiple sources)*

1   2   3   4   5   6   7   8   9   10

Professional Development *(recognition, achievement, accountability, advancement)*

1   2   3   4   5   6   7   8   9   10

Chapter Eleven   Roadmap to Success

Note: Using a separate piece of paper record your answers to the following questions. Take your time when forming your answers, notice emotions, thoughts and gut feelings. If something doesn't "feel" right, investigate why. When forming your answers, be thorough, don't hurry.

This is NOT a race to see who gets done first

This is YOUR life.

1) What do you want to change or achieve? Be as specific as you can. Laser beam type focus is needed to change desire into reality.

Example: I want to make more money!

The above example will NEVER work. Why? Because the stated desire isn't specific enough...How much money? By what date? Doing what to get it? Spending how much time to achieve this? Desire must be LASER beam specific.

2) Reframe stated desire into a positive statement.

Other people's affirmations don't work. For an affirmation to work it MUST come from within yourself to be believable. Better yet, ask yourself a question, THEN write the affirmation from the answer you receive!

3) *What are you willing to do to achieve the desired result?*

Most people will say "ANYTHING", but is that really true?

Think about what you are really willing to do LONG TERM to meet your goals. To be successful you must plan 1-3 years in advance. What can you do NOW to guarantee success in 1-3 years? Are you willing to change your lifestyle? Let go of old behaviors and triggers?

4) Using the 4 "W"s and an "H", i.e. Who, What, Where, When and How.

Specifically design your plan. Be as detailed as you can.

Who can help your achieve this? What actions will you take? Where will you make the changes? When will you make these changes? How will you make these changes?

5) *List the first 5 actions needed to achieve desired result.*

Example for weight loss:

Start an exercise program i.e. walking.

Start a food journal

Change cooking and eating habits

Become more aware of healthy choices in food

Do self hypnosis everyday to promote mental changes

6) What resources will you need to achieve the first five actions? Do you have those resources? If not, what will it take to gain those needed resources? Again, be specific. Breakdown actions to small focused steps for each item. Follow breakdown "trail" all the way to the end.

Using the above example;

Start an exercise program....

Will you exercise at a gym or at home?

Do you need a personal coach or trainer?

If joining a gym, do you have the funds available?

If not, how you plan on obtaining the funds?

If at home, what/who will keep you motivated?

7) Reprioritize the first five actions needed to achieve desired results.

Rethink your order of importance

Rewrite them in the new order

8) How will you know when you have achieved the first five actions? How will you benchmark, acknowledge and record your results? Write down your plan to acknowledge your achievements.

9) *List the next 5 actions needed to achieve the desired result.* List the next five action items needed to be successful.

10) Repeats steps #5 through #9 until desired outcome is reached.

11) Write your steps (action list) needed for your life script using as much detail as possible. Notice your emotions as you are writing your script.

Using the above information, write a script to follow, a recipe for success every day.

You can refer to this script often to stay focused on your outcome.

Pay attention to your emotions as you write this.

any hesitation or conflict.

Is your script believable to you?

Is it doable?

WILL you commit to doing this?

Listen to that little voice inside, notice what it is saying.

Why do you feel that way?

What are your fears?

How will life change?

At this point it may become necessary to review your five steps and make any needed changes.

12) What will achieving this outcome do for me? Again, be specific.

When you reach your goal, what will it do for you?

How will your life change?

What will change for you?

Again be realistic and specific.

Think of family, friends, peers, will they treat you the same and be willing to accept the new you?

Will you treat them the same after your growth?

13) What would happen if I got this outcome with the other important areas of my life? Specifically.

Look at the other areas in your life.

What will reaching your goal do to these areas?

Family, Social, Career, Time, Lifestyle?

14) Would achieving this desired outcome hurt anyone else?

By reaching this goal, will anyone be hurt by it?

Think about this one hard before you answer. This course takes effort, success demands effort PLUS time to achieve our desires.

Are the people around you prepared to be supportive, understanding when you embark on your path to success?

15) Depending on the answers given in steps 12, 13 and 14, there may need to be changes made to the life script.

If changes to the desired result are needed, return to step 1 and follow steps 1 through 15 again.

Remember there are NO right or wrong answers...

This is YOUR life...

Take your time...

Dare Something Worthy!

I'm not sure who the author was that wrote this but I love the simplicity and wanted to share it with you..

To that author...my hat is off to you!

bear philosophy

bears believe in the simple philosophy

that life was made to be cherished and enjoyed

that it's stupid to worry and sensible to smile

that unpleasant things should be taken in one's stride

(...and not thought about)

and if you've made someone smile they've made your day

and bears believe that life is not about

hatred

fear

or jealousy

but about love

peace

and

happiness

And finally...

The Tao of Pooh Bear

"Promise me you'll always remember...

you're braver than you believe

stronger that you may seem

and smarter than you think..."

A. A. Milne

By doing the simple exercises in this book you have changed

You are no longer the person you were when you began reading

Did you make it to the top of your mountain?

Probably not because we will continue to climb that mountain for the rest of our lives...that's what makes life interesting isn't it?

But you HAVE come far....

You ARE braver...you ARE stronger...you ARE smarter

May you succeed beyond your wildest dreams

May every dream that you have come true

Many Thanks and congratulations,

Ron

Please take a moment and send us YOUR success stories about your experience with the Breakthrough to Success program.

Email them to Islandproductions@camano.net

We'd love to hear from you!

To further your knowledge you may wish to purchase our books,

"Transformations; A Guide to Successful Hypnosis"

Island Publishing 2001

"Can't Get Through: 8 Barriers to Communication"

Pelican Publishing 2003

"Weight No More: The Transformation of You"

Island Publishing 2004

"Breathe Easy: The Stop Smoking Program"

Island Publishing 2004

"Embedded Commands and Power Language"

Island Publishing 2005

"The Science of Hypnotic Seduction"

Island Publishing 2006

"Stage Hypnosis 101—A Stage Performers Guide to the Universe"

Island Publishing 2005

More Books

"How to be a Manifesting S.O.B. (Successful Outstanding Being) w/ Dr Joe Vitale

Island Publishing 2004/2015

CD'S

Heart's Journey (Considered for 7 Grammy Awards 2003)

Weight No More Weight Loss System

Breathe Easy: the Stop Smoking System

Release (Taking out the mental garbage)

Mind Cleanse (Taking back control of your life)

Lift Scripts (Success)

Doesn't Have to Hurt (Pain)

Remember When Memory Enhancer (Memory)

Sleep NOW (Insomnia Program)

Boost YOUR Confidence (Confidence Enhancer)

Science of Hypnotic Seduction

Stress Buster

Drifting

Magic Happens (Working with Children)

All products, books and CD's are available on our websites

Ron Stubbs is available for lectures and consultations on Success Coaching, Motivation, Peak Performance, Body Language, Communication, Taking back Control of your Life and a variety of other subjects.

Ron is also available for personal coaching, hypnosis instruction, private therapy sessions in person or by phone, and interviews.

He can be reached at Island Productions

360-387-1197 Or by email Islandproductions@camano.net

For programs to help you reach your goals and take back control over your life, please visit our website at www.ronstubbs.com

Ron is also an internationally performing Comedy Stage Hypnotist.

For Stage Hypnosis Shows

Please visit www.rockandrollhypnotist.com

Made in the USA
San Bernardino, CA
21 May 2015